TALKIN' ABOUT MY G-G-GENERATION

Doonesbury books by G. B. Trudeau

Still a Few Bugs in the System
The President Is a Lot Smarter Than You Think
But This War Had Such Promise
Call Me When You Find America
Guilty, Guilty, Guilty!
"What Do We Have for the Witnesses, Johnnie?"
Dare To Be Great, Ms. Caucus
Wouldn't a Gremlin Have Been More Sensible?
"Speaking of Inalienable Rights, Amy..."
You're Never Too Old for Nuts and Berries
An Especially Tricky People
As the Kid Goes for Broke
Stalking the Perfect Tan
"Any Grooming Hints for Your Fans, Rollie?"
But the Pension Fund Was Just Sitting There
We're Not Out of the Woods Yet
A Tad Overweight, but Violet Eyes to Die For
And That's My Final Offer!
He's Never Heard of You, Either
In Search of Reagan's Brain
Ask for May, Settle for June
Unfortunately, She Was Also Wired for Sound
The Wreck of the "Rusty Nail"
You Give Great Meeting, Sid
Doonesbury: A Musical Comedy
Check Your Egos at the Door
That's *Doctor* Sinatra, You Little Bimbo!
Death of a Party Animal
Downtown Doonesbury
Calling Dr. Whoopee
Talkin' About My G-G-Generation

In Large Format

The Doonesbury Chronicles
Doonesbury's Greatest Hits
The People's Doonesbury
Doonesbury Dossier: The Reagan Years
Doonesbury Deluxe: Selected Glances Askance

A DOONESBURY BOOK BY

G.B. Trudeau

Talkin' About My G-G-Generation

AN OWL BOOK · HENRY HOLT AND COMPANY · NEW YORK

Published by Henry Holt and Company, Inc.,
115 West 18th Street, New York, New York 10011.
Published in Canada by Fitzhenry & Whiteside Limited,
195 Allstate Parkway, Markham,
Ontario L3R 4T8.

Library of Congress Catalog Card Number: 88-80158

ISBN 0-8050-0791-1

First Edition

Printed in the United States of America

The cartoons in this book have appeared in newspapers
in the United States and abroad under the auspices
of Universal Press Syndicate.

1 3 5 7 9 10 8 6 4 2

ISBN 0-8050-0791-1

MR. SLACKMEYER, I'LL TRY TO BE BRIEF. I'M JUST A JUNIOR LAWYER WITH THE S.E.C., AND I REALIZE YOU'VE GOT MORE IMPORTANT THINGS TO DO THAN TALK WITH ME.

HOWEVER, WE'VE BEEN GOING OVER RECENT TRANSACTION RECORDS, AND IT SEEMS YOUR FIRM SOLD ALL ITS MERGER-RELATED STOCKS JUST BEFORE THE BOESKY SCANDAL BROKE.

I'M DEAD.

TELEPHONE RECORDS INDICATE YOU TALKED TO BOESKY MINUTES BEFORE YOU SOLD. MY SUPERIORS FIND THAT VERY PECULIAR.

I BETTER CHECK ON THOSE RESERVATIONS.

PERSONALLY, I THINK IT'S ALL A BIG COINCIDENCE.

BLESS YOU.

GB Trudeau

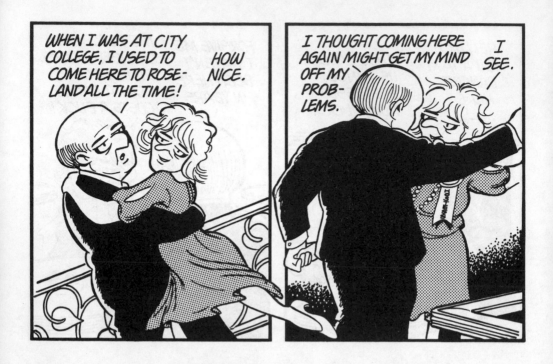

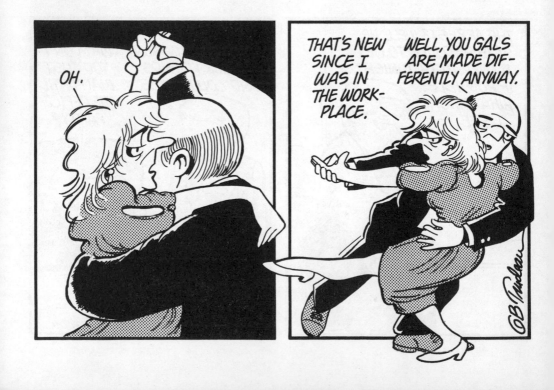

A FEW LIVES AFTER MY INCARNATION AS A HITTITE CONCUBINE, I BECAME A FRESCO PAINTER IN THE MINOAN PALACE AT ZAKRO...

IT WAS MY FIRST LIFE IN THE FAST LANE. I WAS A COURT FAVORITE, AND MADE OUT LIKE A BANDIT UNTIL WE ALL DIED DURING THE ERUPTION OF THERA.

HOWEVER, IT REALLY WASN'T UNTIL MY INCARNATION AS A COURTIER TO QUEEN NEFERTITI THAT I BEGAN TO SEE THE IMPORTANCE OF A SENSE OF SELF-ESTEEM...

PULL IN THAT TUSH, MAJESTY! THAT'S IT! FEEL THE *BURN*!

LADIES AND GENTLEMEN, AS YOU KNOW, FOR THE PAST FEW MONTHS, THE PRESIDENT HAS BEEN MUCH TOO BUSY SETTING THE NATIONAL AGENDA TO MEET WITH YOU ON A REGULAR BASIS.

WE RECOGNIZE YOUR LEGITIMATE NEEDS, HOWEVER, SO WHITE HOUSE TECHNICIANS HAVE RECENTLY CONFIGURED AN ELECTRONIC STAND-IN WHO IS PRIVY TO THE PRESIDENT'S EVERY THOUGHT.

HE CAN BE DEBRIEFED HERE, OR YOU CAN ACCESS HIS FILE, 24 HOURS A DAY, FROM THE COMFORT OF YOUR OWN WORK-STATION. LADIES AND GENTLEMEN, I GIVE YOU MR. RON HEADREST!

YO, PRESS! MIS-MIS-MISTAKES WERE MADE! LIES WERE TOLD! BIBLES WERE SIGNED! SO-SO SUE ME! SUE ME!

©B Trudeau

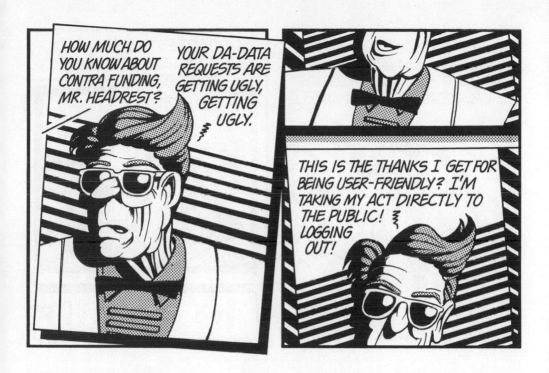

SO HOW DOES HART SOLVE HIS ALOOFNESS P-P-PROBLEM? BY DECLARING AT 11,000 FEET!

I SHOULD TALK! SO I DO! DO! I'M ALL HEART! FROM MY HEAD DOWN TO MY... MY... **HEY!** WHERE'S THE REST OF ME?

HELP ME OUT! I C-C-CAN'T DO THIS BY OURSELVES! YO! HOME BOY! ANY QUES- TIONS?

YES. AM I BEING BILLED FOR YOU?

NO! I'M NOT AVAILABLE IN YOUR AREA YET! YET!

GB Trudeau

NOW, NOW, T-T-TAKE JOE BIDEN! HE'S 45, BUT LIKE HART, 50, HE **SWEARS** HE'S A B-B-BABY BOOMER! ARE THESE GUYS PUSHY OR WHAT? OR WHAT? HOLD IT, BETTER COOL OFF...

I DON'T WANNA SAY MY HOME BASE CIRCUITRY IS H-H-HOT, BUT I JUST GOT PROPOSITIONED BY A LINEAR PHASE CERAMIC MICROFILTER!

THAT RE-RE-REMINDS ME! **KIDS!** NEED ROCK-SOLID INFORMATION ON SAFE SEX? CALL THIS NUMBER ON YOUR SCREEN!

(202) 456-1414

THAT DOES IT.

RING! RING! RING! RING! BBRING! RING! RING! RING! RING! RING! RING! RING! RING! RING! RING!

R.H.

HI. I'M SAL DOONESBURY, AND I'D LIKE TO WELCOME YOU TO THE INSTITUTE FOR IMMACULATE CONTRACEPTION, POPULARLY KNOWN AS WHOOPEE U.!

AS DISTRICT SALES MANAGER TRAINEES, YOU ARE HERE TO LEARN THE WHOOPEE WAY OF LIFE. IT MAY BE THE MOST IMPORTANT COURSE OF INSTRUCTION YOU EVER TAKE!

WHEN YOU SELL DR. WHOOPEE, YOU ARE SELLING HOPE. YOU BECOME PART OF THE SOLUTION. YOU'LL BE SAYING NO TO A MYRIAD OF SOCIAL PROBLEMS!

OF COURSE, YOU'LL ALSO BE WINNING FABULOUS PRIZES!

SAL, HOW MANY POINTS FOR THE CATCHER'S MITT?

©B Trudeau

BEFORE WE START, LET'S TAKE A LOOK AT THIS MOTIVATIONAL VIDEO MESSAGE FROM DR. WHOOPEE'S FOUNDER AND CHAIRMAN!

CLIK!

YOU KNOW, WHEN I FOUNDED DR. WHOOPEE LAST YEAR, I SWORE MY PRODUCTS WOULD BE THE FINEST AVAILABLE ON THE MARKET! WELL, I DELIVERED ON THAT PLEDGE.

HOW DO YOU KNOW? HOW DO YOU KNOW OUR LINE IS ALL I SAY IT IS? HOW DO YOU KNOW WE USE ONLY THE FINEST MATERIALS CURRENTLY AVAILABLE ANYWHERE IN THE CARIBBEAN BASIN?

TRUST ME.

GBTrudeau

AS THE DOG DAYS SET IN AT THE IRAN-CONTRA HEARINGS...

...AND THE ATTENTION OF THE NATION BEGINS TO WAVER...

THE TEMPO PICKS UP WITH THE UNSCHEDULED APPEARANCE OF...

...A SURPRISE WITNESS!

ON THE ADVICE OF COUNSEL, I'LL T-T-TAKE THE FIFTH! NO, NO, THE DINETTE SET! AND THE TRIP TO HAWAII, HAWAII!

...AND I TOOK THESE SLIDES SHORTLY AFTER MY CAMERA-MAN BURT GOT FRIED BY A LIVE SYNAPSE NEAR OUR BASE CAMP.

WHERE ARE WE, MR. HEDLEY?

IN THE CORTEX, SIR. AS YOU CAN SEE, THE IRAN-SCAM MEMORIES ARE WELL-PROTECTED...

... BY AN AWESOME ARRAY OF DEFENSE MECHANISMS. BY MY COUNT, THE PRESIDENT HAS NO FEWER THAN 23 VERSIONS OF THE TRUTH INSULATING HIM FROM REALITY!

CLIK!

23? BUT WE'VE ONLY HEARD... COUNSEL?

FIVE, SIR.

IT COULD BE A LONG SUMMER, SENATOR.

GBTrudeau

THIS IS ROLAND HEDLEY WITH THE BUSH CAMPAIGN IN IOWA...

THE FIRST CAUCUS IS STILL MONTHS AWAY, BUT THERE'S GROWING CONCERN HERE THAT GEORGE BUSH'S FAILURE TO SHOW A POLITICAL PROFILE—**ANY** POLITICAL PROFILE—IS STARTING TO HURT.

TOP AIDES NOW ADMIT THAT BUSH IS SO ADAMANTLY OPPOSED TO BECOMING HIS OWN MAN THAT HE IS IN IMMINENT DANGER OF DISAPPEARING ALTOGETHER!

GBTrudeau

BUSH im '88

HMM... MAYBE A DIFFERENT NECKTIE...

WHAT'S WRONG WITH MY TIE?

A SMALL CROWD GATHERS...

NO PUSHING, P-P-PLEASE! DOWN IN FRONT! THANK YOU, YOU!

MY NAME IS RON HEADREST, AND I'M RUNNING FOR PRESIDENT! IF ELECTED, I WILL **PERSONALLY** TOUR EVERY CHIP USED TO B-B-BUILD STAR WARS, WARS!

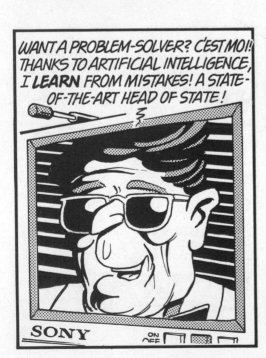

WANT A PROBLEM-SOLVER? C'EST MOI!! THANKS TO ARTIFICIAL INTELLIGENCE, I **LEARN** FROM MISTAKES! A STATE-OF-THE-ART HEAD OF STATE!

SONY

ON OFF

WHAT IF YOU DEVELOP A GLITCH DURING A NUCLEAR SHOWDOWN?

HEAD OF S-S-STATE! STATE! S-S-S-STATE! STATE! WHAT?

©B Trudeau

WORD SPREADS QUICKLY THROUGH THE CONSUMER ELECTRONICS SHOW...

SOMETHING *BIG* IS HAPPENING OVER AT THE SONY BOOTH!

SO FAR HE'S APPEARING ON THE TRINITRON EXCLUSIVELY!

DO YOU THINK THE JAPANESE HAVE A LOCK?

CAN I GET BACK TO YOU? THERE'S SOME SORT OF COMMOTION IN AISLE 23!

YES, FOR J-J-JUST PENNIES A DAY, I COULD BE YOUR PRESIDENT!

GBTrudeau

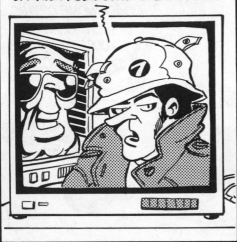

THIS IS ROLAND HEDLEY. TODAY THE BIZARRE VIDEO PHENOMENON KNOWN AS RON HEADREST KICKED OFF HIS PRESIDENTIAL CAMPAIGN.

BEFORE A RAPTUROUS AUDIENCE OF IOWAN VIDEO ARCADE OWNERS, HEADREST GAVE A LONG, INCOHERENT SPEECH, THE GIST OF WHICH...

WA...ZT! PHZZT! WHPSZZ!

GIST, MY FOOT! ROLL TAPE!

GBTrudeau

MY S-S-STRATEGY? WELL, I THINK I'LL KICK THE CAMPAIGN OFF BY PANDERING TO THE FAR RIGHT, RIGHT!

IF THE PIONEERING WORK OF GEORGE BUSH IS ANY INDICATOR, THEN STROKING THE CRAZIES IS *K·K·KEY* TO PRIMARY SUCCESS!

BUT, MR. HEADREST, IF YOU VEER TO THE RIGHT, HOW WILL YOU EVER APPEAL TO THE INCREASINGLY CRITICAL BLACK AND HISPANIC VOTE?

NO P-P-PROBLEM.

HEADREST BECOMES THE CON-SUMMATE G.O.P. CANDIDATE.

♪ YIP, YIP, YIP, YIP, YIP, ⚡GET A **JOB!** SHA-NA-NA-NA-SHA...

HE IS, AT ONCE, DEFEN-DER OF THE FAITH...

...AND OPPORTUNITY FOR **ALL** AMERICANS—WHITE AND BLACK, RICH AND POOR, WHITE AND RICH!

...SCOURGE OF THE SPEND 'N' BORROW CROWD...

IT'S T-T-TIME WE **PAID** AS WE WENT, SENATOR! IT'S TIME FOR **CABLE** GOVERNMENT!

©BTrudeau

...AND COMMITTED FAMILY MAN.

I'M HOME, HONEY, HONEY!

MISS BOOPSTEIN? WE'D LIKE TO THANK YOU AND MR. HUNK-RA FOR A **SUPER** AFTERNOON!

MY FRIENDS AND I ARE CONVENTIONEERS FROM TENNESSEE. FRANKLY, WE WERE A BIT SKEPTICAL ABOUT CHANNEL-ING.

BUT YOU'VE TURNED ALL OF US INTO BE-LIEVERS! COULD YOU AUTOGRAPH THIS PIC-TURE OF YOU FOR OUR GROUP?

SURE! THE NAME AGAIN?

THE ILLEGITIMATE DAUGHTERS OF ELVIS.

GBTrudeau

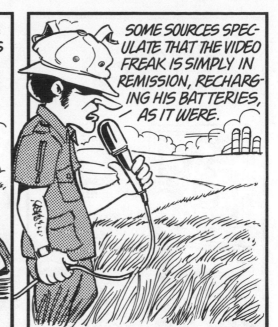

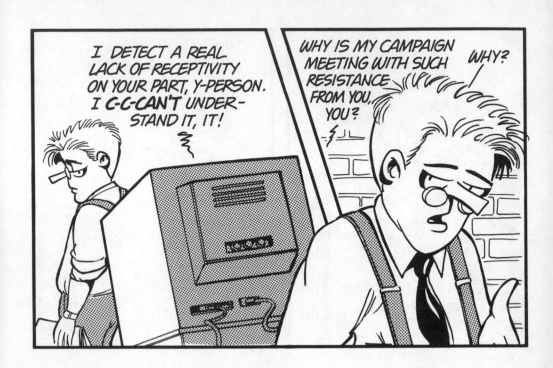

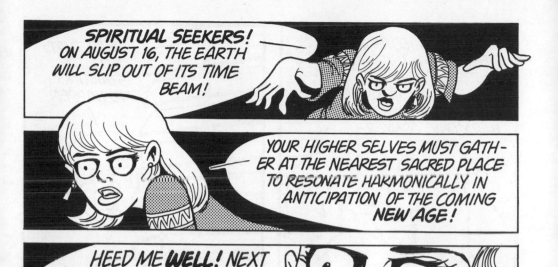

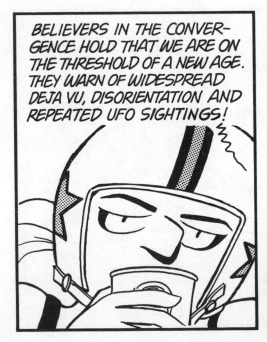

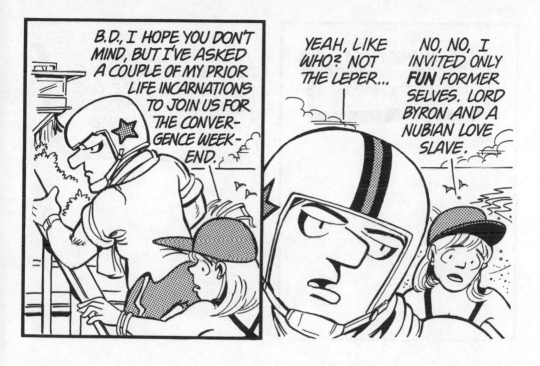

HARMONIC CONVER-
GENCE: MANKIND'S
SECOND CHANCE.

IT IS WRIT LARGE, SOME-
WHERE: "IN THE CUSP OF
CONVERGING AGES, ONE
BLINDING, HOLY MOMENT
OF TRANSCENDENCE...

... SHALL TRANSFORM THE
ZEITGEIST WITH PERFECT
SYNCHRONICITY, INTO THE
PURE, INEFFABLE EXPRES-
SION OF INDIVISIBLE...

...ONENESS."

OH, RIGHT! YOU
WERE EXPECT-
ING ARTWORK
OF *THAT*?

SOME SORT
OF SUNSET
MIGHT'VE
BEEN NICE.

NOTHING! **NADA!** SOME HARMONIC CONVERGENCE!

NO DISORIENTATION! NO DEJA VU! NO INVITATIONS TO JOIN A FEDERATION OF EXTRATERRESTRIALS! A TOTAL **BUST!**

BOOPSIE, I TRIED TO TELL YOU. SOMEWHERE IN THE WORLD PEOPLE MAY BE GETTING IT ON WITH THEIR DIVINE SPARKS...

...BUT **NOT** IN PALM SPRINGS!

I CAN'T UNDERSTAND IT. IT'S ON THE LIST OF SACRED ZIP CODES!

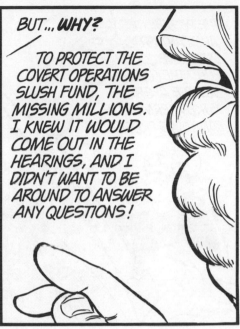

DUKE, LET ME COME RIGHT TO THE POINT...

I'M ALL EARS, BILL!

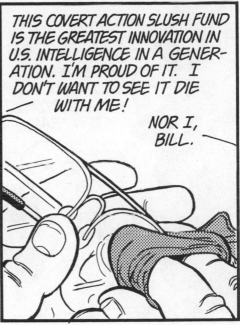

THIS COVERT ACTION SLUSH FUND IS THE GREATEST INNOVATION IN U.S. INTELLIGENCE IN A GENERATION. I'M PROUD OF IT. I DON'T WANT TO SEE IT DIE WITH ME!

NOR I, BILL.

I NEED YOUR HELP, DUKE. I NEED SOMEONE WHO CAN LEAD THE ILLEGAL COVERT OPERATIONS OF THIS COUNTRY INTO THE TWENTY-FIRST CENTURY!

GEE, I DUNNO, BILL. I GOT A LOT ON MY PLATE AND...

CLIK!

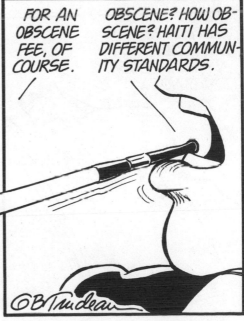

FOR AN OBSCENE FEE, OF COURSE.

OBSCENE? HOW OBSCENE? HAITI HAS DIFFERENT COMMUNITY STANDARDS.

©B Trudeau

I'M ROLAND HEDLEY. HERE AT A PHOENIX SHOPPING CENTER, THE MOVEMENT TO RECALL ARIZONA GOVERNOR EVAN MECHAM IS PICKING UP STEAM!

WHY? WELL, IT ALL STARTED WITH HIS RESCISSION OF THE STATE'S MARTIN LUTHER KING HOLIDAY. EVER SINCE, CRITICS SAY, MECHAM'S RECORD HAS BEEN POCKMARKED BY INSENSITIVITY.

THE GOVERNOR, UNDERSTANDABLY, BEGS TO DIFFER...

IT'S LUDICROUS! I'M A MORMON! TOLERANCE IS A BASIC TENET OF MY FAITH!

SO THE CHARGES AGAINST YOU...

LIES! LIES SPREAD BY QUEERS AND PICKANINNIES!

I'M DONALD TRUMP, AND I'M **NOT** RUNNING FOR PRESIDENT!

I'M JUST A BILLIONAIRE DEVELOPER EXERCISING HIS RIGHT TO FLOAT TRIAL BALLOONS!

IF I **WERE** RUNNING, THOUGH, IT'D BE AS AN ORIGINAL, AS A BELOVED ARCHETYPE—THE AMERICAN LANDLORD!

EVERYONE ♥'s A LANDLORD!

UH... EVER HAD ONE, SIR?

NO, BUT I'M TOLD HE'S KIND OF A FATHER FIGURE.

MR. TRUMP, YOUR DENIALS NOT-WITHSTANDING, DON'T THE ADS YOU TOOK OUT SUGGEST A TEST-ING OF THE POLITICAL WATERS?

AS I HAVE SAID BEFORE, I WAS SIMPLY ACTING AS A CONCERNED CITIZEN!

AT THIS TIME, I HAVE **NO**, REPEAT **NO**, POLITICAL AMBITIONS WHATSOEVER!

OKAY, BUT IF YOU **DID** RUN FOR CONGRESS...

PRESIDENT. THINK PRES-IDENT.

OKAY, LET'S TAKE A LOOK AT THE C-C-CHARACTER SCORE-BOARD! IT'S ONLY OCTOBER, AND THE BOYS OF WINTER ARE ALREADY **TWO DOWN!**

AND THAT DOESN'T EVEN INCLUDE **PAUL LAXALT**, WHO D-D-**DIDN'T** SUSPEND HIS CANDIDACY FOR CHARACTER REASONS, BUT **SHOULD** HAVE, HAVE!

OF COURSE, NOW THAT HE'S OUT OF THE RACE, THERE'S **NO** POINT IN RETELLING THE STORY OF P-P-PAUL'S "NEVADA PROBLEM"!

OH, WHAT THE HECK! 1983: LAXALT GOLFING PARTNER AL DORFMAN IS RUBBED OUT IN A SUBURBAN PARKING LOT...

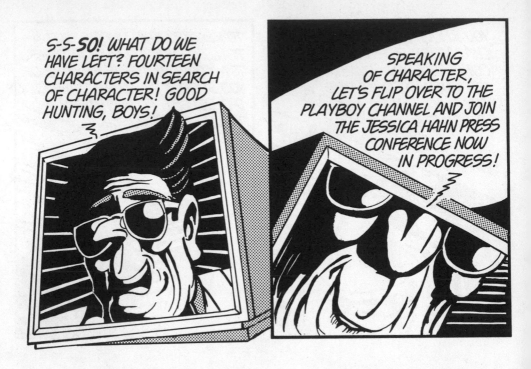